A Guide to
AMERICAN ANTIQUE FURNITURE

A concise, simplified study of the styles and periods of American furniture, with most of the articles of antique furniture particularly described and illustrated so as to enable the reader to identify them.

A Guide
to
American Antique Furniture

By

Gustave A. Van Lennep, Jr.

With Illustrations by

Vida S. Van Lennep

1937

Macrae · Smith · Company

PHILADELPHIA

COPYRIGHT, 1937, MACRAE · SMITH · COMPANY
All rights reserved

3710
Manufactured in the United States of America

✻ Contents ✻

	PAGE
Foreword	vii
Chairs	15
Chests of Drawers	29
Chests-on-Chests	35
Highboys	39
Lowboys	43
Desks	47
Secretaries	53
Serving or Sideboard Table	59
Sideboards	63
Tables	67
Settle and Settees	73
Sofas	79
Beds	83
Clocks	87
Mirrors	91
Prices	95

✷ Foreword ✷

ALMOST everyone has heard something about antique furniture, for it becomes more popular every day. Few, however, have more than a bewildered idea about the subject or know more than a few isolated names. Furthermore, there is at the time of writing no work on the subject which is comprehensive enough to give a picture of the whole field and which was not written for the collector or student. To gain any useful knowledge about American antique furniture, to recognize and appreciate the styles of the old periods requires a great deal of study in works that do not invite study by the beginner. It is the purpose of this work, therefore, to give an introduction to this fascinating field by presenting a comprehensive view of the whole subject, giving in each period the characteristic style points and then more particularly describing in some detail most of the pieces of furniture which may be found in many American homes today. In this way, at least, enough will be learned to allow the reader to recognize typical pieces, to place the period in which the style originated, and to acquire the orientation in the whole subject which will make any further study that may be contemplated so much easier.

The illustrations are all sketches and as such are not intended to more than convey the idea of the style or form of the piece described in the text. This is a work for the beginner and not the collector. It has been impossible in such a large subject to cover every known piece of antique furniture. Rather only more typical pieces are described to better clarify the styles of the various periods. But styles change slowly, and many pieces exhibit the characteristics of several periods, when they are called transitional pieces. Thus a chair may have the cabriole legs with pad feet of the Queen Anne period and the top rail and back of the Chippendale. It must not be imagined that transitional pieces are less desirable than pure pieces. Once the typical characteristics of each period are mastered, the reader should have no trouble in recognizing the transitional piece.

We shall deal with six great periods, which because of certain characteristics of form and style have given their names to the furniture which was made at that time. If a piece has the points and style of a certain period, it is described as of that period. Hence, a chair made in the middle 18th century, having certain style points first introduced or developed by Chippendale and characteristic of his pieces will be called a Chippendale chair; not necessarily because Chippendale himself made the chair, but because it is made in the Chippendale style. There are thousands of pieces of furniture made in the style of Chippendale which are called for convenience Chippendale, whereas Chippendale himself made only a very small part of them. The same is true of all the periods, which take their names either from the ruling monarch of the country during the time when the style developed or from the cabinetmaker who introduced or popularized the style. Hence, we speak of William and Mary furniture, which exhibits styles made popular during the reign of William and Mary in England, Queen Anne furniture after the Queen of England in whose time the styles were set, or Chippendale, Hepplewhite, Sheraton, names of the great cabinetmakers who introduced, popularized, or executed certain styles.

The six periods, with approximate dates, are: William and Mary, 1688-1710; Queen Anne, 1710-1750; Chippendale, 1754-1780; Hepplewhite, 1786-1800; Sheraton, 1790-1810; Empire, 1810-1830.

The dates are only relatively important, because of course no period begins or ends abruptly in any given year. Styles change gradually and carry over from one period to the next in transitional pieces, to die out slowly or perhaps be revived at some later time. Chippendale and Hepplewhite were contemporaries, but Chippendale is considered earlier in the history of style changes because his styles became popular soon after the publication of his book of designs in 1754, "The Gentleman and Cabinet Maker's Director," whereas Hepplewhite's designs did not become popular until after his death in 1786, when his work was published for the first time by his widow.

For those who wish to make a more exhaustive study of the subject the following works can be recommended: "Furniture Treasury," by Wallace Nutting, published by the Old American Company, Framingham, Massachusetts, the most complete collection of photographs on the subject ever compiled; "Blue Book of Philadelphia Furniture from William Penn to George Washington, with Special Reference to the Philadelphia Chippendale School," by William MacPherson Hornor, Jr.

We wish to acknowledge the very helpful advice and criticism given by David Stockwell in the preparation of this book.

A Guide to
AMERICAN
ANTIQUE
FURNITURE

CHAIRS

In dealing with the parts of a piece of furniture, certain more or less technical names have for convenience come into general use, and as they carry an exact and well understood meaning will be used wherever necessary. Thus in discussing chairs, the following terms will be used:

Stiles are the side pieces that support or form the frame of the back, usually continuing in one piece into the back legs below the seat.

Finials are small ornamental carvings or turnings in the shapes of balls, flames, or other patterns which top or terminate the stiles of a few chairs and more commonly decorate the tops of large cabinet pieces, as highboys or secretaries.

The *splat* is the central vertical member of the back, usually shaped or pierced and carved with openwork.

The *top rail* is the horizontal rail or cross piece that forms the top of the back, while the seat rail is a similar piece that forms the front of the seat frame.

The *stretchers* are horizontal cross pieces that join the legs, used to strengthen the legs.

Early Chairs

* WAINSCOT *

THE term Wainscot is applied to these early chairs, mostly made before 1700, because the back is panelled and sometimes the sides, and even below the seat rail to the feet, much like the wainscotting or panelling of a wall. Oak was most commonly used in the English Wainscot chair, but in America walnut is the usual wood. These chairs are more solid and substantial than beautiful, but have a certain dignity of their own. In rare instances they are decorated with carving on the top rail and seat rail, but usually they are plain.

* BREWSTER *

THE Brewster is a rather elaborately turned chair with beautifully turned spindles in the back and below the seat rail in front. The back is high, as the illustration shows, often with balls on the arm posts and deeply turned finials on the stiles. The arm joins the stile at a right angle, while stretchers are double, turned, and low to the ground. The seat is usually a rush or reeded seat, though solid wood seats are found. In America the Brewster chair was usually made of maple and hickory.

The Carver chair is found during the same period, about 1690, and is very much like the Brewster, only being distinguished by the absence of spindles in front below the seat.

* SLAT BACK *

Also called the Ladder Back, this is a turned chair with a slat back and rush seat. The back is high and may have from four to six slats. The illustration shows the arm posts topped with mushrooms, and ball finials on the stiles. Legs, stiles, and stretchers are always turned, usually in ball patterns. These chairs may or may not have arms. As we approach the time of Queen Anne some appear with cabriole legs, and the slats are cut into arches. The ball foot is used extensively. Many variations exist in these chairs. The earliest appear about 1700, and in America they were made until as late as 1850. Around 1700 the front stretcher was elaborated with the deeply turned ball which gradually disappears, while the plainest were made in the 19th century.

* BANNISTER BACK *

These chairs first appeared around 1690 and were not made after 1725. They have a high narrow back like the slat back chair, but in the place of slats the back is composed of upright pieces called bannisters, set straight up and down in a frame. As in the illustration, there are usually four bannisters in number, and often more, and they may be flat thin pieces or turned. Sometimes the top rail is elaborately carved, but more often it is plain, rather flat, wide, and scalloped or cut into scrolls. There are usually deeply turned finials on the stiles, and the feet are commonly turned balls. The seat is rush, but may also be wood.

[16]

* FLEMISH *

THESE are the narrow high back chairs, with or without arms, and with elaborate turnings on the top rail and stretchers, that were popular during the William and Mary period; i. e., about 1700. They are called Flemish because the Flemish scroll is the usual carving and appears on the top rail, the back panel, and often on the front stretcher and foot. The illustration shows how elaborately carved some of these chairs were. Notice the foot, called the Spanish foot, which was used in this and the next period, Queen Anne. The ball foot and variations of it is perhaps commoner in the William and Mary time. The seat and back are usually caned, as in the illustration, or in leather, while a few appear upholstered. The wood was usually maple, and fruit woods were also used, as well as walnut for the finer chairs. These are the chairs so often seen today, in reproductions, as the formal chairs in halls and reception rooms.

* WILLIAM AND MARY *

As WILLIAM was Dutch, one would think that the Dutch styles would appear at this time. The Dutch influence does not make itself so apparent in furniture, however, until later, in Queen Anne's time. The typical William and Mary points are the trumpet and the inverted cup turning, and the ball foot. There are no chairs which have these characteristics in pure enough form to be called William and Mary chairs. Instead the Flemish and the turned chairs described above were popular at that time.

* QUEEN ANNE *

THE illustration shows the Queen Anne side chair, which is most typical of the period. It appears with the cabriole leg and drake foot. Another foot, even more typical of the period, is the Dutch or pad foot. The cabriole leg is most characteristic of the period and was popular all through the 18th century. It may be described as a gracefully curving leg, somewhat like a flattened "S" curve. This leg only appears in front as the back legs on all chairs are plain, with a few rare exceptions in richly carved chairs.

The back of the Queen Anne chair, as can be seen, is rounded, and the splat shaped and usually cut out to resemble a large urn, often with scrolls or volutes carved on the sides.

Stretchers tend to disappear from the legs at this time. The arms are nicely curved outward, and round down into the posts. The typical Dutch foot later in the period is varied with the claw-and-ball foot, which in turn becomes so popular in the Chippendale time. In the later Queen Anne chairs the leg is often carved at the knee with a shell, and a shell may appear in the skirt under the seat rail and also in the center of the top rail. The seats are fully upholstered or slip and often have a skirt which may be scalloped. These were made at least until 1750, when they disappear before the popularity of the Chippendale chairs.

The three feet typical of the Queen Anne period are illustrated. The first is the Spanish foot, so-called because it originated probably in Flanders when that state was under Spanish rule in the 17th century, and came in with the Flemish styles. It appeared first around 1700 or earlier and was used with the cabriole leg in the Queen Anne period, though it is not so common as the other two types.

The second from the left is the drake foot, so-called because it has three toes joined somewhat like a duck's foot. This foot also appears on the cabriole leg through the Queen Anne time and is typical of the period.

The foot on the right is the Pad or Dutch foot and is most typical of the Queen Anne period. It is called the Dutch foot because it came in with the Dutch styles in England in the first part of the 18th century.

[18]

* CHIPPENDALE *

CHIPPENDALE chairs are deservedly popular and are the best examples of the designs of this famous craftsman, called the greatest of the English cabinetmakers. The chair illustrated at the left shows the typical cabriole leg with ball-and-clawfoot, and shells carved on the seat rail, top rail, and knees. The most characteristic carving in the Chippendale time is the acanthus leaf, which is used elaborately on the richer pieces. The back legs are unadorned and sweep outward as in the Queen Anne chairs. The back is high and expanded or flared, usually with rolled ears, and the splat is made up of gracefully intersecting curves and scrolls, open work of the finest sort. The stiles are sometimes fluted in front, and the splat carved elaborately, as in the Philadelphia types which are the richest made in America.

As Englishmen travelled to the Orient in the latter half of the 18th century, the Chinese influence began to come in and resulted in what are called the Chinese Chippendale types. In chairs this took the form of square, untapered, straight legs. The chair illustrated is this later type. The leg was plain at first, then molded, and later becomes adorned with delicate open-work brackets and incised carvings, and appears with the block foot. The seat is always upholstered in these chairs, and some arm chairs have upholstered backs.

With the Chinese influence, bamboo turnings (wood turned to look like bamboo) began to appear in the later Chippendale time. These later Chippendale chairs with the square untapered legs are unique and always can be identified, as there are no others quite like them. They have a pleasing solidity which is not overly heavy or ungraceful.

[19]

* HEPPLEWHITE *

ALTHOUGH contemporary with Chippendale, Hepplewhite is considered later because his designs came into popularity after Chippendale's. He published no book during his lifetime, as did Chippendale, so his work was not known until after his death in 1786, when his book of designs, "The Cabinet Maker and Upholsterer's Guide, or Repository of Designs for Every Article of Household Furniture in the Newest and Most Approved Taste," was published in 1789 by his widow, Alice Hepplewhite, who carried on the business.

The illustration shows a Hepplewhite side chair of the shield back variety, the most common type of Hepplewhite chair. The splat or center of the shield is open work of a variety of delicate patterns: urns with flowers, feathers, drapery, etc. The seat is sometimes hollowed, sometimes flat, and the front is usually a suppressed serpentine curve. The seat when upholstered is often outlined with ornamental tacking, and slip seats are common. The legs are slender and delicate, square, tapering to the foot which is usually spade, as illustrated. The spade foot is truly typical of Hepplewhite. Often the legs are fluted or molded, and sometimes, together with the front rail, are inlaid with a white wood, usually satinwood, in fine lines and patterns. The shield back side chair with its delicacy and grace typifies Hepplewhite, together with the use of fine inlay.

* SHERATON *

SHERATON and Hepplewhite have in common a certain delicacy of line, and undoubtedly Sheraton was influenced greatly by the Hepplewhite styles so popular when he began designing. There are many transitional pieces, and the two are often confused.

The Sheraton chair illustrated is typical, with its straight turned legs, usually reeded as shown, and with the turned foot. The seats are upholstered or caned, usually with a square front, but sometimes the front takes a slight serpentine curve. The back is typically square, and indeed it may be said that the square back labels the Sheraton chair, though the older tradition of the square, tapered

Hepplewhite leg persisted for long. The turned reeded leg is purely Sheraton. The back is delicately carved with variations of the urn, festoons, and patterns of classical influence. In the unupholstered chair, the seat rail is often reeded and decorated with carving, and in the arm chairs the arms often rise in a graceful curve almost to the shoulder, as the back is short compared to the Chippendale chair.

As the period progressed, the chairs grew slightly decadent and were often painted with conventionalized floral and fruit motives. The lines were less fine, the construction cheaper and inferior. From this time on, through the Empire period, there is a great decline in taste and a poverty of ideas. The pieces become heavy and ornate, while grotesque carvings such as heavy animal feet, dragon's heads, pineapples, and other motives take the place of beauty of line and form.

There are excellent craftsmen still at work, however, and Duncan Phyfe is the outstanding example in America at this time. Working in New York, he employed a hundred men, and so there are many pieces made by him. He followed the Sheraton and later the Empire styles, and used always the best examples of each, but did not create any new designs or styles which can be called Duncan Phyfe. His work achieved a distinction of its own, however, through his use of the best styles in vogue combined with a certain originality of carving and handling of material. Many pieces are erroneously called Duncan Phyfe when it is meant that they are executed in the best late Sheraton or Empire style. The chair illustrated shows Duncan Phyfe's technique. Called a Lyre Back chair, this piece might well have been made by Duncan Phyfe. The design marks a blending of Sheraton and Empire styles. Only pieces made by Duncan Phyfe should bear his name, since he is responsible for no particular style. We speak of chairs as Chippendale which are patterned after the designs created, introduced, or developed by Chippendale, and of course he did not make most of the chairs which bear his name. And so it is with the other great designers, Hepplewhite and Sheraton. But in the case of Duncan Phyfe and other great cabinetmakers who worked in the style of the period in which they lived, like John Goddard, Benjamin Randolph, and William Savery, we apply their names to the pieces they are supposed to have made in their own shops.

The Federal Period is a commonly heard designation. This period dates in America from the time of Washington's election to the presidency, in 1789, to about 1815. The Hepplewhite, Sheraton, and Empire styles were followed generally.

* EMPIRE *

The styles of the Empire period came in as a direct result of Napoleon's conquest of Egypt, which inspired the Empire motives along with the other classical influences of the day. At first the styles were based on classical precedent, but later were combined incongruously to produce many grotesque forms.

As the late Sheraton grows into the Empire period, the back of the chair begins to swing outward or roll. The legs also follow this tendency to flare outward, while the arms complement the sweep of the back with a roll at the posts. The legs are slightly tapered and may be heavily reeded or plain, and often they are turned.

Later the top rail becomes quite wide with carved ears flat on the face, and the carving becomes poor in the workmanship, but remains ornate. Often the back has only one carved piece or slat parallel to the top, heavily and ornately carved. The animal foot appears quite commonly, and grows larger and heavier as time goes on.

The chair illustrated is a model quite common in the Empire period, but the styles are so varied that no one chair can be designated as typical.

* HITCHCOCK *

This is a late Sheraton or Empire chair so called because first made in the town of Hitchcock, Massachusetts. It came into vogue through the popularity of the late Sheraton painted chair. It has round turned legs and a rush seat, and the front stretchers may also be turned. The outline of the back is square, while the top rail is turned with a pillow in the center, as the illustration shows. Painted decorations appear on the stiles, top rail, and legs. The central part of the back may be painted with the usual motives of the Empire period, cornucopias, fruits, flowers.

No one set of characteristics can describe the style of the Empire period. There are a tremendous variety of patterns and kinds of chairs. But the spirit of the age is reflected in the furniture to a marked degree: lack of moderation and extremes in line and contour which grows grotesque in the heavier pieces. It is very easy to identify an Empire piece by this feeling.

* WINDSOR *

The Windsor Chair was made principally in the latter half of the 18th century. Though the design originated in England, named after a type appearing in Windsor Castle, the American Windsor is a more graceful and pleasing chair. The English Windsor lacks character in that the legs do not flare, the back does not bow so fully, the arms do not curve so gracefully as does the American Windsor.

The seat of the Windsor chair is made from one solid piece of wood, pine or poplar, hollowed out to form a saddle. The deeper this hollowing is the better. The legs are turned, usually in the vase pattern, and are driven into holes bored through the seat. This is done while the wood of the seat is unseasoned or green, and as the wood seasons it shrinks upon this already very tightly fitted leg to form a practically permanent joining of the leg and seat. The leg is made of maple usually and the spindles in the back and arms of hickory.

The illustration on page 23 shows a Comb Back Windsor, so-called because the effect of the spindles passing through the center rail and then held together at the top by the top rail is that of a lady's comb of the period. The more of these whittled or turned spindles in the back the better. The top rail, as can be seen, is lightly serpentined and scrolled at the corners, giving the effect of ears. In the chairs without arms of this type with the serpentined top rail, the arm rail disappears, of course, and it is called a Fan Back Windsor, because it now resembles a fan more than a comb. The Fan Back seems to differ in appearance from the Comb Back only in the absence of the arms and arm rail around the back.

Even commoner than the Comb Back is the Bow Back Windsor as illustrated, called a Bow Back because the back is formed by a piece bent around in the shape of a bow. The chair illustrated has arms held or connected by a rail running around the back and is more specifically called a Sack Back Windsor, from its similarity in shape to a sack. The Balloon Back is another popular name for a Windsor which, having a bow back and arms, lacks the arm rail. In this type the arms are tenoned into the bow, or in the New England chairs the bow is bent to form the arm all in one piece.

After the Chinese influence made itself felt in the late 18th century, bamboo turnings were used in Windsor chairs quite commonly. Windsor chairs are almost never found with rockers. But the Boston rocker, somewhat resembling a Windsor, was a very comfortable and popular rocking chair made around 1830. It has a wide top rail, spindles in the back, a rolling arm, and a wide rolling seat, deeply curved to fit the body.

The square lines of the Sheraton influence appear in Windsors around 1800. Usually there is a slight curve or bow in the top rail and sharp corners at the ears. Often there is a medallion in the form of a small rectangular piece with the corners curved set in the top rail at the center. (See the illustration of the Windsor settee.)

* WING *

THE Wing Chair is first found around 1700. The finest types are found in the Queen Anne and Chippendale times. As the drawing shows, the Wing chair is a completely upholstered chair with high sides like wings, whence it derives its name.

The Queen Anne Wing chair as illustrated usually has the cabriole leg, shortened, with the Dutch or pad foot. The leg is usually plain and there may be a turned stretcher or no stretcher at all. The arms roll horizontally or vertically as the case may be. Often a combination of these is found, as in the illustration, the vertical extending from the seat rail, and the post curving outward in a "C" curve at the arm, which rolls horizontally. This is the finest form.

The Chippendale Wing chair has the cabriole leg with ball-and-claw foot. The knee is often carved with the acanthus leaf or shell, and sometimes the skirt is carved, as in the richly finished Philadelphia chairs. Later Chippendale Wing chairs have the square, untapered, straight leg which is often molded, reflecting the Chinese influence.

In the Hepplewhite time the back is often taller, and the wing consequently longer, though the old proportions are followed pretty faithfully in general. The top of the back is sometimes serpentined, as are the wings on the taller models. The square, slightly tapering leg is used.

The Sheraton Wing chair has the same form in general with the turned reeded legs as the distinguishing feature. After the Sheraton period the Wing chair becomes very heavy.

CHESTS OF DRAWERS

IN EARLY times the plain chest or large box was used to keep clothing in. A bottom drawer was added, and finally, about 1690, the piece became entirely composed of drawers as we know it.

The early chests of drawers were of oak, but very soon in America pine, poplar, maple and walnut came to be used. These early William and Mary pieces have a panelled front and molding around the drawers. The fronts and ends are, in rare instances, elaborately decorated with painted flower motives, as the tulip. As the legs disappeared with the increase in the number of drawers, the large ball foot became popular, though the turnip foot was also used as well as carrot with a shoe under, all resembling the respective vegetables.

The chests of drawers are always flat-topped, and the tear drop brasses are typical in the William and Mary period as drawer pulls, though wooden knobs were also used. Early in the 18th century very much taller pieces appear, though the lower chests were made all through the century and are usual after the Chippendale time.

* QUEEN ANNE *

THE feet in the Queen Anne time are the tall bracket feet, almost square. The bracket tends to be plain at first and then becomes more elaborate, with scroll or scallop work. Sometimes short, bandy cabriole legs are used with a Dutch foot, but these are not graceful with the usual heavy cabinet piece and are not common.

* CHIPPENDALE *

THE illustration shows a straight front Chippendale chest of drawers. At this time curved fronts also appeared, the curve taking several forms. The serpentine curved front is common and may be described as having a bulge or swell in the center, a curve inward or depression about where the handles appear on the drawers, and a slight return curve outward at the corners.. (See the Sheraton chest of drawers for illustration.) The oxbow front is another curved front appearing at this time and is just the reverse of the serpentine; that is, it goes inward at the center and out at the handles or brasses and then makes a return inward and straightens at the corners. (For illustration see the Chippendale Secretary.)

With the oxbow and serpentine fronts the corners of the chest of drawers are sometimes chamfered, or bevelled, and may be fluted or carved on the chamfer, but more often plain. Quarter columns are often set into the corners of the Chippendale chest of drawers, and this is shown in the chest illustrated. The drawers are usually made with a very fine molding on the edge, called a lip-edge or overlapping drawer, because when closed the drawer fits flush with the front with the molding overlapping. Later a beaded edge drawer appears near the Hepplewhite time.

The feet in the Chippendale time are most commonly the bracket foot with the double cyma or ogee curve, called ogee feet. This is illustrated on the chest of drawers shown, and is the most graceful foot for the low heavy cabinet pieces. The ball-and-claw foot is also found, especially in New

England, but is not so pleasing because it requires a cabriole leg which in these low cabinet pieces had to be too short to be graceful.

The block front also appears at this time and was developed largely by John Goddard, a cabinetmaker of Newport, Rhode Island. These fronts are easy to recognize, having square or rounded blocking extending outward or in relief at the ends over the brasses. The top is usually shaped to fit the contour of the front. A large shell is often carved at the tops of the drawers, and ogee bracket feet are most commonly found on the block front type.

* HEPPLEWHITE *

THE Hepplewhite chest of drawers is mainly characterized by fine inlay work and the taller bracket foot, curved slightly outward, called the French bracket foot. The piece illustrated is a typical Hepplewhite chest of drawers. The handles or brasses are oval shaped, and the drawers are outlined with inlay work. The skirt, in addition to being shaped as shown, may be scalloped more elaborately and curve gracefully downward at the center. The swell front illustrated is typical, and the straight front also was used, as in all periods.

* SHERATON *

THE Sheraton chest of drawers is much like the Hepplewhite, except that the turned reeded leg is used. Reeding is the opposite of fluting and may be described as the effect obtained by tying a bunch of reeds together in a round form. Fluting is cutting out with a half round instrument below the surface.

The Sheraton chest of drawers illustrated shows the turned

reeded leg carried up the side in a column, as in the rarer types. This column may be decorated in the later pieces with carving, following the fruit and floral motives of the time. The swell and straight fronts are most common, though the serpentine front, illustrated, is also found. The round brasses shown are typical of the period, though the older oval brasses continue to be used. On smaller Sheraton chests of drawers are often mirrors on stands with small drawers under the glass, like the older shaving stands.

* EMPIRE *

THE Empire chests of drawers are heavier and more highly decorated than the Sheraton pieces. The legs are heavily turned, usually with casters, and the side columns have deep spiral carvings called the Archimedean screw, in architectural language. The acanthus leaf also appears again in the carving, and other floral designs, elaborately executed. Often the top drawer is set out to overhang the lower drawers, and the glass knob handle comes into use on the drawers. Heavy veneering is used with nicely-matched oystering effects. The large animal foot is common.

CHESTS-ON-CHESTS

THE chest-on-chest is well described by its name. These pieces arose evidently from a demand for more clothing space than the ordinary chest of drawers afforded. They first appear in the Queen Anne period and continue principally through the Chippendale time. The chest-on-chest is made in two pieces with a molding on the top of the lower piece to retain the upper section. The backs of the two pieces are usually flush, with the sides and front of the upper piece an inch or two smaller than the lower part.

On the earlier pieces, in the Queen Anne time, the short bandy cabriole leg appears, usually with the Dutch or pad foot. The tall straight bracket foot is more usual, however, in the Queen Anne time. Often the skirt is scrolled and decorated with sunbursts or shells at the center. The top is usually flat at this time, although some bonnet top pieces are found.

In the Chippendale period the chest-on-chest is commonly found with the scroll or bonnet top. The illustration shows the scroll top chest-on-chest of the Chippendale period. The scroll top is flat in section, rather like a false front, and is broken at the center with a central figure, as an urn or flame finial. Flame and ball finials are almost always used at the base of the scrolls and on the bonnet tops. Rosettes are often carved in the roll ends of the scroll, and dentils (teeth-like carvings), also appear under the cornice and along the scroll.

The lower section is similar to the chest of drawers with fewer drawers and has the same characteristics in corresponding periods.

The bonnet top, as illustrated under secretaries, extends the full width of the top like a hood and is shaped like the scroll top from a front view. It has the same kind of central figure in the break of the scrolls, and finials and other decorations in the same manner. The chest-on-chest grows less common after the Chippendale period.

HIGHBOYS

THE highboy grew out of the earlier chest on frame, drawers being added to fill in the chest. As more space was required the piece grew taller, until it reached almost to the ceiling in the later pieces. The top part, which contains most of the drawers, is set into the frame and is removable.

In the William and Mary period the highboy appears as illustrated, flat-topped, straight front, and turned legs with flat stretchers close to the ground. The drawing shows the typical inverted cup turning in the legs, and the usual ball feet, here with pads. The trumpet turning is also typical in the William and Mary period and is illustrated in the William and Mary lowboy. Notice the drawer handles, called the tear drop brasses, which also mark the William and Mary piece.

The early highboys were occasionally decorated with painted tulips and other flowers, and when the piece was made of soft wood, like pine, it was sometimes entirely painted. The drawers usually have a molding around the edges and fit flush with the front when closed.

The legs vary from four to six in number, the front having two or four as the case may be with only two in the back. The sides are sometimes panelled, and arches appear in the skirt, often with the full arch in the center as in the illustration. After the six-legged type began to disappear and four legs took its place, a drop (a turned ornament of some kind, the reverse of a finial) was attached to the skirt at the points where the extra legs had been attached. This is shown in the William and Mary lowboy illustrated.

In the Queen Anne time, the cabriole leg appears on the highboy, with the pad foot. The flat top is still most common, though later in the period the bonnet top appears. The front and skirt may be decorated with shells or sunbursts, and there is often a large shell or fan on the front at the top between the smaller drawers, as in the chest-on-chest illustrated. After about 1740 and through the Chippendale period the usual tops are the scroll and bonnet tops.

In the Chippendale period the highboy reaches the height of its development and disappears altogether at the end of the period. The use of carving, often elaborate, becomes more general. The scroll or bonnet top is often very elaborately streamered and carved, with an urn, vase with flowers, or other ornament between the scrolls.

The illustration shows a Chippendale highboy with scroll top and flame finials, fluted quarter columns set into the corners of both top and lower sections, and cabriole legs with ball-and-claw feet. This is the typical Chippendale highboy. The legs tend to grow more squatty on the taller pieces, and are often carved on the knee in the finer pieces with a shell or acanthus leaf. The skirt is often carved with shells, sunbursts, rosettes, and other designs. At the top, the cornice may be decorated with dentils and frets under. The brasses are the typical willow pattern of the Chippendale time. At the height of the Chippendale period the finest furniture in America was being produced in Philadelphia, richly carved and of the most excellent workmanship, by such master craftsmen as Benjamin Randolph, William Savery, Thomas Affleck, and others.

LOWBOYS

The lowboy was made to match the highboy and was used originally as a lady's dressing table. In 1700, William and Mary, it appears as illustrated, with the typical leg of that time (the trumpet turned leg), and with the ball foot. Crossed stretchers, flat and close to the ground, are also typical. The drawers, as in the case of the lower section of the highboy, were usually arranged as shown, two deep drawers at either end of the frame, and a small shallow drawer in the center, with an arch or scallop work underneath in the skirt. The typical William and Mary tear drop brasses were used for drawer pulls as shown. Sometimes a finial appears at the intersection of the crossed stretchers.

* QUEEN ANNE *

In the Queen Anne lowboy the stretchers disappear, and the cabriole leg with the Dutch or pad foot is used. The Spanish and drake foot is also common. The skirt is usually scrolled or arched in the center with the full Queen Anne arch, and often a shell or sunburst appears under the small center drawer. The arrangement of the drawers is now usually as shown, with a top drawer the full width of the front and two deep drawers under at either end with the small drawer in the center. Later a shell is sometimes carved on the knee of the cabriole leg.

✱ CHIPPENDALE ✱

IN CHIPPENDALE'S time the carving and decoration grow more elaborate. The foot is a large, deeply carved ball-and-claw, and the acanthus leaf is carved on the knee of the cabriole leg in the richer pieces. As the illustration shows, the small center drawer gives way to a large deep drawer in the center, often carved with shell and sometimes streamers, lines of applied carvings.

The side corners are sometimes chamfered and fluted or, as in the piece illustrated, fluted quarter columns may be set in. A cove or hollow molding also appears around the top. The Philadelphia lowboy again reaches the height of elaboration in carving and workmanship. These later richly-decorated lowboys were used also as side tables and for many other purposes out of the bedroom.

[44]

DESKS

The desk originally was a box, which was carried around and set on the knee. The box was later set in a frame with a slant lid. The illustration shows an early desk, which has the lid hinged at the top so as to swing up instead of down. The legs are tall and usually turned, as in the lowboy, with flat crossed stretchers close to the ground in the William and Mary period. The early American pieces were made of pine often, with maple stretchers and frames. A strip molding sometimes appears on the slant lid to serve as a bookrest. The button foot is common, and stretchers are sometimes spool-turned and may run through the middle. Some of the desks are all in one piece, and some are set in a frame—removable.

* WILLIAM AND MARY *

IN THE William and Mary period, the slant lid soon is hinged at the bottom and swings down to form a flat writing surface, supported by slides. The drawers also begin to increase in number, finally reaching almost to the floor. The ball foot is typical, with a turned leg which grows shorter as the number of drawers increases. Tear drop brasses are also typical as drawer pulls in the William and Mary pieces. Walnut and maple were used in America for these cabinet pieces.

* QUEEN ANNE *

IN THE Queen Anne desks with the drawers solid to the feet, the typical feet were the tall, straight bracket feet. Other Queen Anne desks appeared with fewer drawers, and these had usually the graceful cabriole leg with the customary feet of the period, the Dutch or pad foot, the drake, and the Spanish foot. (See the illustrations of these feet under Queen Anne chairs.) On the more solid models, the short, bandy cabriole leg with the pad foot is sometimes found, but this foot is ungraceful and not so pleasing as the bracket foot on the heavy cabinet piece.

CHIPPENDALE

The New England Chippendale desks usually have the ball-and-claw foot, but the bracket foot comes into general use at this time in the Middle Atlantic and Southern states. This may be a straight bracket or curved with the double cyma or ogee curve, called the ogee bracket foot. With the drawers almost to the ground, this is the most graceful foot for the heavy cabinet piece.

The desk illustrated is a Chippendale slant-top desk, with ogee feet, the typical Chippendale willow pattern brasses, and fine interior, with shells carved over the small drawers at the top. Carving and the use of decoration becomes apparent, and the skirt under the drawers is sometimes embellished with a shell. Fluted quarter columns may be set in, or the corners may be chamfered and fluted.

The interior of the desk is decorated with blocking, carving, and serpentining of the small drawers. The acanthus leaf and shell are the usual motives for the carving, and scalloped or shaped trim appears over the pigeon holes at the top. Sometimes half-round columns are found on either side of the document drawers, and secret drawers became popular.

The straight front is most common, but the curved fronts begin to appear in the Chippendale time, taking the form of the serpentine and oxbow curves. See the description of the curved fronts under chests of drawers. The block front also appears, used often with the knee-hole desk, which is flat-topped. In the knee-hole desk the front is recessed or cut in deeply for the knees, and it usually has the block front in the Chippendale time.

* HEPPLEWHITE *

The Hepplewhite desk is distinguished by the use of delicate line inlay around the drawers and on the corner posts. The slant top and drawer fronts are commonly veneered. The oval brasses are typical, and so is the tall, gracefully curved bracket foot, called the French bracket foot.

In the Hepplewhite period appears the Tambour desk, which is illustrated. This is a very dainty piece, with slender tapering square legs and often spade feet, as in the illustration. The writing surface is made by the flat top hinged in front and supported on slides when opened. The tambour is the flexible covering over the inside of the desk, which rolls back into the sides when opened. This is made of thin, half-round slats, glued to cloth.

* SHERATON *

The typical Sheraton desk is a bureau type, although the slant top is still used occasionally until the Empire period. The flat top Sheraton desk looks much like a chest of drawers. Round turned legs and feet are usual, as are the round brasses. The front of the top drawer lets down to form the flat writing surface.

* EMPIRE *

The desk, along with other furniture, grows heavier in the Empire period. It is flat-topped and of the bureau type. The large top drawer pulls out, and the front drops down to form the writing surface, with the usual small drawers and compartments inside the drawer. The use of columns at the corners the entire height of the piece becomes common, and these may be heavily carved. The feet are usually the massive animal feet of the period.

SECRETARIES

The lower part of these pieces is exactly like the desk of the corresponding period, with the upper section set on the flat narrow top and apparently designed for books. The earliest styles are found in the William and Mary period, when it has the usual ball feet, a square top, molding or beading around the drawers and top, and tear drop brasses.

* QUEEN ANNE *

The Queen Anne secretary is rather plain at the top. The doors may be panelled, often with the Queen Anne arch, a full half-round arch with the ends carried off at right angles. The most common foot at this time is the bracket foot, which is tall and square at first and then becomes curved, with the ogee bracket foot becoming popular around 1750 in transitional pieces. The bandy cabriole leg with Dutch foot is sometimes found on the secretary at this time, but is not common. Towards the end of the period, or close to the Chippendale time, the top begins to be developed, the bonnet top appearing first as in the highboy.

* CHIPPENDALE *

In the Chippendale period the top becomes fully developed on the secretaries. The scroll and the bonnet tops are both prevalent. The Chippendale secretary illustrated has the scroll top, with the oxbow front. Notice how the oxbow front of the desk proper terminates at the top in so-called breast drawers. The doors are panelled and shaped at the top to correspond. The feet are the typical ogee feet. Another top found at this time is the Pitch Pediment top, which is a purely classical motive. Usually the pediment is broken like the scroll and bonnet tops with some central figure or finial. The bonnet top illustrated on the next page has flame finials and shows clearly the form of this common top of the Chippendale period. The pitch pediment top is also illustrated above the bonnet top.

In the upper section fluted quarter columns are sometimes set in the corners, or the corner posts may be flat and fluted, or chamfered and fluted or carved. The interiors of the tops are often very fine, and candle slides, which pull out from the base of the top, are common.

* HEPPLEWHITE *

The taller French bracket foot (see illustration of Hepplewhite chest of drawers) appears on the secretary in the Hepplewhite period, and the legs grow taller while the number of drawers in the base decreases. The square, tapering leg is characteristic of Hepplewhite, often ending in the spade foot, as shown on the Tambour desk. Delicate line inlay is used around the drawers and often on the legs. The oval brasses are typical, though round brasses appear also.

The slant top disappears at this time, and the pediment of the upper piece becomes simpler, being sometimes delicately scrolled, often with open work in the scroll. Usually it is almost flat, as in the Sheraton secretary illustrated on page fifty-five, with three high points or plinths, upon which are mounted brass finials. An eagle is sometimes mounted in the center, with brass finials in the shape of balls or vases at the ends. The writing surface is formed by a flat piece hinged to the flat top of the lower section, which when turned down rests on slides. Glasses appear in the doors, set in delicate square or diamond-shaped frames or muntins.

* SHERATON *

The illustration on page 55 shows a typical Sheraton secretary, distinguished from the Hepplewhite by the turned, reeded leg, and with cathedral-shaped glasses in the doors of the upper part. The round brasses are also more characteristic of the Sheraton than the Hepplewhite period, though they appear on Hepplewhite pieces. Often, as in the desk, the top drawer pulls out, and the front lets down to form the writing surface. The corner posts are sometimes reeded in front, and the glass in the doors is held by delicate muntins or frames, in cathedral, diamond, and other shapes. The top remains much the same as in the Hepplewhite time, with the three brass ball or urn-shaped finials, mounted on small pedestals. Sometimes the center figure is an eagle.

* EMPIRE *

THE Sheraton and Empire styles mix early in the secretary. The later Empire secretaries become heavy and ornate. Large animal feet appear, and columns are carried up the sides. Heavy veneering is also characteristic. Round glass knobs are used as drawer pulls in the place of brasses.

SERVING OR SIDEBOARD TABLE

Before the Hepplewhite period (1790) the sideboard was not in use. Instead the sideboard table was used in the dining room, also called a serving table. These were flat tables, often with a marble top. The Queen Anne sideboard table has the cabriole leg, often with the pad foot, and often a scalloped or scrolled skirt.

In the Chippendale period, the ball-and-claw foot is early used, followed a little later generally by the square, untapered leg with the block foot. The illustration shows this later Chippendale serving table with the square leg of the Chinese influence. Often the square leg is molded and may be combined with Chinese fret work in the apron, with open brackets at the legs.

The Hepplewhite sideboard table has the typical square, delicate, tapering legs of the period with the usual fine line inlay on the edges and around the drawer. Sometimes the front is serpentined.

The Sheraton sideboard table complements the sideboard and is smaller and purely a serving table. The round, turned, reeded leg is characteristic.

SIDEBOARDS

With the advent of the Hepplewhite styles about 1790, the sideboard first came into use. Longer than the sideboard table, the sideboard usually has six legs, four in front and two in back. The illustration shows a richly inlaid sideboard of the Hepplewhite period. The brasses are the oval pattern, and the use of inlay in fine delicate lines and the bell and cornflower motives is characteristic. The front is serpentined in the center, while the ends are concave and the top drawer swell shaped. The typical slender, tapering legs are usual. Sometimes a tambour cupboard is found below the long drawer in the center. As described before, the tambour is a flexible covering made of thin splints split in half and glued to cloth. It rolls back into the sides on opening, like the roll-top desk of modern times.

The Sheraton sideboard, illustrated, is distinguished from the Hepplewhite by its turned, reeded legs, and the cabinet shows a tendency to grow closer to the floor at the ends as the legs grow shorter. The reeding is often carried up from the legs onto the pilasters above each leg. The straight front, combined with a swelled center section, is often used and takes the place of the concavity found at the ends of the Hepplewhite sideboard. Perfectly straight fronts are found commonly in both periods. Fine veneering and oystering also mark the Sheraton sideboard, while round brasses are typical.

The Empire sideboard grows more massive and less graceful. The legs often continue as columns to the top, turned with heavy spiral reeding, and sometimes carved at the top with a pineapple.

Cupboards appear under the single flat drawers at the center and ends, and the piece is solid to the floor. The shape is now like the modern sideboard as we know it. The feet are turned with flower and fruit motives, which appear more or less in the carving on the columns. These columns also exhibit Ionic and Corinthian capitals. The carving generally tends to be in large masses and elaborate. Beautiful veneering is achieved, and the top of the sideboard sometimes has a high and elaborate railing around it, heavily carved, and often holding a mirror. The ends also go up, and the top becomes broken in the center on this type.

TABLES

* WILLIAM AND MARY *

THE dining table found in the William and Mary period was an oval top table, as illustrated, with turned legs and stretchers. This table is called a gate leg table, because the leg swings out to support the drop leaf and resembles a gate, with its stretcher low to the ground and cross piece at the top. The turnings are commonly the ball, the sausage, or the vase patterns, and the common foot is the button foot. The table illustrated has the vase turnings. Maple, cherry, and walnut were commonly the woods used, with maple pieces appearing early in New England.

* QUEEN ANNE *

THE Queen Anne dining table remains oval generally, with drop leaves. Stretchers have disappeared, though the legs still swing out to support the drop leaves. The cabriole leg is characteristic, with the pad and sometimes the Drake foot. Often the apron is scalloped at the ends of the frame.

* CHIPPENDALE *

IN THE Chippendale time the oval table is still in use, but the square or rectangular table soon comes into style. The table illustrated is a Chippendale dining table with cabriole legs and ball-and-claw feet. Sometimes the leg is carved on the knee with a shell or acanthus leaf. With the square tables, the square, untapered leg is often found, usually with the block foot. The square top is popular because it enables two tables of the same height to be placed end to end to form a larger dining table. Walnut and mahogany are the usual woods used in America for the dining table at this time.

* HEPPLEWHITE *

The Hepplewhite dining table has the slender, square, tapering legs, often with fine inlay work along the edges and across the lower part of the leg. The spade foot is sometimes found. These tables are often made in pairs, round or oval at one end and straight at the other, so as to fit together to form one large oval table. A rectangular table was sometimes made to fit in the center to make an even larger dining table, called a three part table.

The Sheraton dining table has the turned, reeded legs so characteristic of all the Sheraton pieces. Sometimes a brass socket appears at the foot, with a caster.

* EMPIRE *

In the Empire time spiral turned legs first appear, and then the pedestal leg type, often reeded along the tops of the legs and with three or four legs to the pedestal. The illustration is of a popular standard or pedestal base dining table, a style so often used by Duncan Phyfe early in the Empire period that this table is commonly referred to as the Duncan Phyfe dining table. Later the heavy Empire styles come in, with elaborate carving, large animal and dragon feet, and large pineapple carvings at the base of the pedestal sometimes.

* TAVERN TABLE *

There are many kinds of small occasional tables in all periods, and a few of the more important types will be briefly mentioned. From the latter half of the 17th century and through the William and Mary period the tavern table was used in halls and parlors. Because it was commonly seen in taverns and inns, it was called a tavern table. It was a small rectangular table with turned legs, stretchers close to the ground, and button feet. A drawer in front was also usual.

During the Queen Anne period, small occasional tables appeared with graceful, slender cabriole legs; pad, drake, or Spanish feet, and scalloped skirt.

✳ TRIPOD AND TILT TOP ✳

IN THE late Queen Anne and all through the Chippendale time small tripod or pedestal tables, usually called tea tables, were common, and several of the type are illustrated. The table with the top tilted forward, at the right, has the slender, typical snake feet; while the table on the left shows a larger tea table with the top in place. Notice the cage at the top of the pedestal, which usually appears on the tilt-and-turn table. This allows the top to revolve. The larger ball-and-claw feet are also typical on this Chippendale type.

Similar tripod tables, called candle stands, were used in the parlors beside chairs to hold candles for reading. These were smaller than the tea table, and the top was tilted or fixed as in all the pedestal tables.

✳ PEMBROKE ✳

THE Pembroke table was a small rectangular table with drop leaves and a drawer. According to tradition, it was first made for Lady Pembroke in the Hepplewhite time, but it ranges in style from the Chippendale through the Sheraton periods. In the Chippendale time the Pembroke table has the square, untapered legs; while in the Hepplewhite the legs are typically the tapering, square legs of the time. The illustration shows a Hepplewhite Pembroke table with oval drawer pull. The turned, reeded leg becomes characteristic in the Sheraton time. These tables were used for a wide variety of purposes in parlors and halls.

* CARD *

CARD tables are found in all periods, and have the corresponding characteristics of the time. They were drop leaf tables with four legs, one of which swings out to support the leaves when open. A typical Sheraton card table is illustrated, with the usual turned reeded legs of the period. The fronts are often serpentined and sometimes elaborately decorated with inlay.

SETTLE AND SETTEES

Settle

THE settle is the forerunner of the settee. It was made, as illustrated, with the back, arms, and front below the seat solid and often panelled. Sometimes the back is very high, and hooded to keep the draught away and hold the heat in. The seat board was sometimes hinged to form a box or chest and also might be lowered to make a deep bed when filled with feathers. The wood used was oak, though walnut and occasionally pine are found. Later the settle appears with the arms open. Both the wainscot chair and the settle are of the same time, both usually being made before 1700.

Settees

The settee is a bench with a wooden or cane back, distinguished from the sofa in that the back is not upholstered, whereas it always is in the sofa.

* QUEEN ANNE *

The Queen Anne settee, illustrated, is like two or more arm chairs joined together and has the same characteristics as the Queen Anne side and arm chairs: cabriole legs, Dutch feet, rounded back, splat shaped like a large urn, arms curving gracefully outwards to meet the curved armposts, and upholstered seat, often slip. The small settees, like the two chairs joined, are called love seats.

* CHIPPENDALE *

In the Chippendale time, the settee is still two or more chairs joined together and has the same style points as the Chippendale chairs: the ball-and-claw foot on a cabriole leg, which may be carved on the knee with the acanthus leaf; square-shaped back flaring out at the corners, with carved top rail and rolling ears; pierced splat made up of gracefully intersecting curves, and upholstered seat. The straight leg comes into use later, as in chairs, and may be molded or carved with Chinese fret.

* HEPPLEWHITE *

The Hepplewhite settee has the typical shield back of the Hepplewhite chair, and other points are the same: square, delicate, tapering legs, perhaps with the spade foot; the use of fine inlay of satinwood; and upholstered seats, sometimes outlined with ornamental tacking on the settees without slip seats. The chair backs tend to lose their separate identity as chair backs joined by a common seat, and the top rail becomes continuous on some pieces, curved or straight, and flowing into the arms.

* SHERATON *

IN THE Sheraton period the square back is typical, and so the straight top rails of the chairbacks in the settee tend to consolidate themselves into a straight single back. The turned reeded leg and more elaborate carvings of the splats and top rail with festoons, urns, flowers, draperies, etc., mark the Sheraton settees just as they characterize the chairs. The fancy painted Sheraton settee with the rush or cane seat or plain wooden seat comes late in the period, and corresponds to the Hitchcock chair.

* WINDSOR *

THE Windsor settee is made like the Windsor chair, with turned legs driven into the seat, which is solid or of one piece, and spindles making up the back and arms. The illustration shows a Windsor settee of the Sheraton period, with the square back and bamboo turnings so characteristic. Note the medallions set in the top rail, also found in Windsor chairs of the Sheraton time. The number of legs may vary from four to ten or more.

* EMPIRE *

IN THE Empire period the settee is scarcer and plainer because the sofa outmoded it. The legs are turned, and the seat usually made of wood, though occasionally upholstered. Rush and cane seats are also found. The top rail is wide and flat, often with painted decorations, as flowers, leaves, and other floral motives. The back is often open except for one flat center slat.

SOFAS

The sofa is an all upholstered piece as distinguished from the settee. It first appears as such in the late Queen Anne period, when it has the Dutch or drake foot, and later the ball-and-claw foot, on the short but graceful cabriole leg.

* CHIPPENDALE *

IN THE Chippendale period the cabriole leg may be carved with a shell or acanthus leaf at the knee. The back may be scrolled gracefully, and the arms roll horizontally and sometimes vertically like the arms of the wing chair. The ball-and-claw foot is prevalent in the Chippendale period, but later the square, untapered leg, often molded, appears with the Chinese influence on styles. The sofa illustrated has the square leg of the Chippendale time with gracefully curved back and arms in the typical manner. These sofas may be short or long, and when short are called love seats.

* HEPPLEWHITE *

IN THE Hepplewhite sofa the arms are thinner, and the back curves more gently. The front may be straight, serpentined, or swell, and there is occasionally some carving on the top of the back at the center. Delicate, square, tapering legs are usually on the Hepplewhite sofa, often with the spade foot, and the use of inlay appears on the legs sometimes.

* SHERATON *

THE illustration on the next page shows a typical Sheraton sofa with the usual turned, reeded legs, so characteristic of Sheraton, and the square shaped back. The arms are thin and delicate and no longer have any roll. Often the upholstering stops short of the face or top of the arm, which may be reeded or molded, and curves gracefully into

the arm post. The arm post is usually turned with urns or vases and is reeded. The top rail is usually unupholstered and decorated, as shown, with carvings of draperies, festoons, thunder-bolts in Duncan Phyfe pieces, and baskets of fruit in Samuel McIntyre's, famous cabinetmakers of this period.

* EMPIRE *

IN THE Empire period the sofa, like most other pieces, becomes heavy and ungraceful. The frame is much heavier in back, and the arms tend to roll outward in a goose-neck shape. Often fan or cornucopia patterns are carried out on the face of the arm. Heavy carving of fruit and floral motives appears all along the face of the arms, skirt,

and back. The legs are squatty and massive, with the large animal feet so typical of the period, combined with ornate foliage brackets.

The illustration shows a fairly graceful early Empire sofa, with animal feet well executed, but very much plainer than the sofas a little later. The Duncan Phyfe sofa may have more delicate legs, with brass feet and casters, curving sharply outwards somewhat like the legs of a pedestal table.

BEDS

THE early beds, when space was limited, were often of the folding type which could be concealed in the cupboard or collapsed against the wall. The former was called the press and the latter the folding bed. Space was saved by the use of trundle beds for children, which were low enough to go under the large standing bed in the daytime. Some of the earliest beds were built into the wall.

At first the bed was entirely enclosed by a canopy, both to keep out the cold and for privacy. After the canopy disappeared from the front and sides, the top and back were still enclosed, and the tradition of the high posts, our "four-posters," remained after all canopy had gone out of use. In the fully canopied bed the posts were hidden, and so were usually plain and unimportant except as supports for the canopy. But as the drapery disappeared, the front posts and legs were revealed and became decorated, and finally the back posts and legs also as the drapery disappeared entirely.

* QUEEN ANNE *

IN THE Queen Anne time the drapery was still in general use, and although contrary to most fully canopied beds which have the woodwork undecorated, some are found at this time with Dutch or pad feet.

The illustration shows typical bed posts of the Chippendale, the Hepplewhite, and the Sheraton periods in order from right to left.

* CHIPPENDALE *

IN THE Chippendale period, the posts were often round and plain at first, tapering to the ceiling. As the canopy disappeared, the post became fluted and carved, sometimes with the acanthus leaf. Later the square post with block feet appeared, and the ball-and-claw foot was often used with the short, bandy cabriole leg, carved sometimes with the acanthus leaf or shell. Flame finials also appeared at this time on the tops of the posts. The Hepplewhite bed has the square, tapered leg with a large spade foot. The posts are round and reeded usually, often with urn finials at the tops above the canopy frame. Urn turnings with carvings sometimes appear in the posts.

* SHERATON *

THE Sheraton bed has the turned leg and foot. The posts are turned with large vases and urns, and sometimes carving appears, of leaves, vines, and floral motives. Often the Sheraton posts are reeded, as are the legs, and the urns beautifully draped.

The canopy frames take a variety of shapes. The arched canopy is found in all periods, and rises in a gentler curve than the bow-shaped canopy, sometimes called the field or tent bed. In the field bed the posts are semi-high, with the canopy frame curved rather high in a full bow shape, and it is usually found in the Hepplewhite or Sheraton periods. Beds with straight, high posts and testers are found in all periods.

* EMPIRE *

THE Empire bed is very massive, with heavy canopy frames. The posts are turned, heavily reeded, or carved deeply and almost crudely with acanthus leaves, and sometimes a pineapple at the top and base. The legs are turned and heavy. The headboard may be panelled and carved at the top, and footboards come in later in the period. The canopy frame begins to entirely disappear as do the four posts. The Sleigh bed is of the Empire period, about 1830, and has the head and footboard rolling outward like the dashboard of a sleigh.

CLOCKS

* TALL CLOCKS *

WITH the tall or grandfather clocks, the cases have the characteristics of the period in which they were made. The earliest have no feet, or ball feet in the William and Mary style. Brass faces are found on the earlier clocks, the painted face coming in around the time of the Revolution.

The top remains rather plain until after the time of the Revolution, although many are found with finials. As the case was the expensive item in the purchase of the Tall clock, many bought the works separately and hung them on the wall. With the pendulum swinging in full view, the name "wag on the wall" was applied to these clocks. Later the case would be purchased and the works installed.

The tall clock cases are slow to change styles, and the characteristics of one period hang on long into the next. In the Chippendale period, the top soon becomes developed as in the other tall cabinet pieces, like secretaries and highboys. The scroll top becomes characteristic, and is usually broken, with flame or ball finials as in the tall clock illustrated. Ogee bracket feet are also typical of the Chippendale tall clock case, with fluted quarter columns often set in. Usually the door is arched to complement the arch of the top and over the face. Sometimes a decoration appears on the door, as a shell in the finer cases. The clock illustrated is a tall clock of the Chippendale time, with bracket feet after the style of Simon Wallard, a famous clock maker of Massachusetts.

The Hepplewhite influence brought the taller French bracket feet, the use of fine, line inlay and veneered mahogany to the clock case. The scroll top was often inlaid and decorated with rosettes and dentils, and instead of the carved finials the brass ball finials characteristic of Hepplewhite.

The Sheraton changes in the tall clock case were not desirable and were not felt until long after the period ended with other furniture. The feet were heavy and turned, and the base was often panelled. The top became more massive, with tinted rosettes and heavier finials. With the Empire styles, which soon mix with the Sheraton in the tall clock, the case becomes heavier and short and fat. The tall clock goes out of use about 1830.

* SHELF *

There were many kinds of shelf clocks in use in the first half of the 19th century. Perhaps the most pleasing and best known is the type illustrated, usually associated with Eli Terry, a clock maker of the early 19th century in Connecticut. Seth Thomas also made similar clocks at that time in Connecticut. These clocks had wooden works, running on weights for thirty hours usually. This is the best style of case, with delicate bracket feet, slender columns along the face, scroll top with brass finials, and painted historic and decorative scenes on the glass of the door. The face was painted also. This style of case went out about 1830.

* BANJO *

The Banjo clock was a wall clock which came into style in the last part of the 18th century and continued in its best form until about 1820, when it became heavy and degraded in the Empire period. It appeared as illustrated, and takes its name from its resemblance to a banjo. Historic scenes were painted on the glass at the base, and because the naval battle between the "Constitution" and the "Guerrière" was a common scene, these clocks are often called "Constitution clocks."

[88]

MIRRORS

* QUEEN ANNE *

THE typical Queen Anne mirror hangs vertically and is oblong, with bevelled glass usually in two parts. The lower part is longer, and the upper curved or arched to correspond to the top, which is arched and crested, with scroll cut-outs. The frame is usually cross banded with veneer. The illustration shows the typical plain Queen Anne mirror. More elaborate decoration was used on some pieces, with a carved and gilded shell sometimes set in the scroll top, and a gilt mold around the edge of the glass.

* CHIPPENDALE *

THE usual Chippendale mirror has the scrolls at the top and bottom, with cresting of veneered mahogany over some soft wood backing. The glass is plain, of a thin sheet, and in one piece. There may be rather elaborate embellishments, such as a cockle-shell, a carved and gilded eagle or other bird on a plinth on the cresting at the top, or carved and gilded leaf and other floral carvings down the sides.

* HEPPLEWHITE *

THE Hepplewhite mirror is similar in shape to the Chippendale, but appears with more elaborate scrolling. It may be inlaid with shells, line inlay, and exhibit classical influence such as an urn in the cresting, with sheaves of wheat carved and gilded.

* SHERATON *

IN THE 19th century the architectural influence made itself felt on mirrors, and glasses exhibiting columns and pediments became the mode, called often "architectural glasses." These mirrors are hung vertically, and have reeded or fluted pilasters the full length of the frame, often carved more or less elaborately at the top, or exhibiting Ionic capitals. The frame is divided into two parts. The lower part contains the rectangular looking glass; while the upper section contains a painting on glass of some decorative or historic scene, or a reserved panel of finely crotched wood, carved. The simpler of these frames is made of mahogany, and the more elaborate are carved and completely gilded. The illustration shows a typical Sheraton architectural glass or mirror, with the characteristics just described.

In the Empire period the mirrors decline in form and appear with great, bulbous, carved and gilded turnings, such as the mantel mirrors, with heavy, ornate frames decorated with large clusters of plaster figures, gilded.

PRICES

It is meaningless to generalize about the prices or values of antique furniture, because no two pieces are worth the same amount except possibly in the rare instance of a perfect match and even then they might not sell for the same price due to market conditions. It is also impossible to give with any accuracy the value of a specific piece unless that piece has been examined carefully as to its age or authenticity, its condition, whether it has been restored or is all original, and many other factors which only the expert can determine. Also the identity of the maker is important if it can be proved. Thus a Chippendale highboy by an unknown maker might sell for five hundred dollars; while another of almost the same appearance but made by William Savery or Thomas Affleck, famous Philadelphia cabinetmakers, might sell for five thousand dollars. Perhaps the highest prices for antiques were reached at the sale of the famous Reifsnyder collection in New York, when the most prominent collectors were bidding against each other.

All these factors must be considered in determining the value of any antique. But it should be apparent that any authentic antique in proper condition and of a desirable period is valuable, and by describing the various periods it is hoped that the reader will be taught enough to recognize his furniture for what it is.

NOTES